Drew Brees

By Jeff Savage

AMAZING ATHLETES

Lerner Publications Company • Minneapolis

For Jordan Macchia—the Saints fan soon to be catching passes from Drew

Lerner Publications Company
A division of Lerner Publishing Group, Inc.
241 First Avenue North
Minneapolis, MN 55401 U.S.A.

Website address: www.lernerbooks.com

Library of Congress Cataloging-in-Publication Data

Savage, Jeff, 1961–
    Drew Brees / by Jeff Savage.
       p.   cm. — (Amazing athletes)
    Includes bibliographical references and index.
    ISBN 978-0-7613-6652-2 (lib. bdg. : alk. paper)
    1. Brees, Drew, 1979-—Juvenile literature. 2. Football players—United States—Biography—Juvenile literature. 3 Quarterbacks (Football)—United States—Biography—Juvenile literature. 4. New Orleans Saints (Football team)—Juvenile literature. I. Title.
    GV939.B695S28 2011 [B]
    796.332092—dc22   2010014542

Manufactured in the United States of America
1 – BP – 7/15/10

TABLE OF CONTENTS

Drew throws the ball during **Super Bowl** XLIV (44) against the Indianapolis Colts.

SUPER VICTORY

Quarterback Drew Brees ran onto the field with the New Orleans Saints. Drew's team was trailing the Indianapolis Colts by one point,

17–16. Fewer than 11 minutes remained in the 2010 Super Bowl. Drew looked at his teammates in the **huddle**. "Let's be special," he told them.

Drew *(wearing number 9)* talks to his teammates in the huddle.

With four lightning-fast plays, Drew had the Saints 20 yards from the **end zone**. A **field goal** would give them the lead. But Drew wanted a **touchdown**. Passes to Robert Meachem and David Thomas got them closer. Then Drew fired a two-yard pass to Jeremy Shockey for the touchdown! The Saints had the lead. Drew had completed seven straight passes to seven different receivers. With 5:35 left, the Saints were ahead, 24–17.

The Saints were not expected to win the Super Bowl. They were longtime losers. Before this season, they had won only two **playoff** games in 42 years. Could their fairy-tale season really come true? Most of the fans at Sun

Life Stadium in Miami Gardens, Florida, were rooting for them.

The Colts tried to answer. Quarterback Peyton Manning drove his team to the New Orleans 31-yard line. Manning threw a pass to wide receiver Reggie Wayne. Saints player Tracy Porter jumped in front of Wayne. **Interception!** Porter raced 74 yards for a touchdown. New Orleans won the Super Bowl, 31–17.

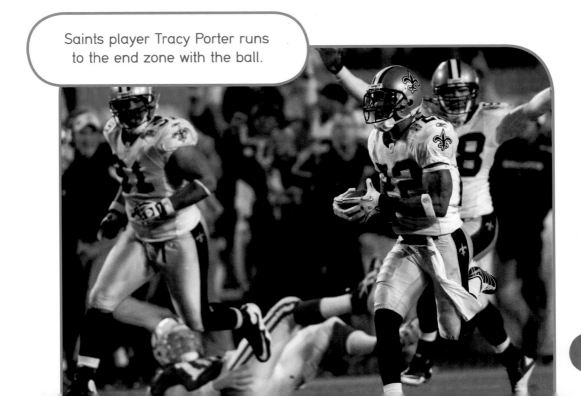

Saints player Tracy Porter runs to the end zone with the ball.

The Saints celebrated. Drew was named the Most Valuable Player (MVP) of the Super Bowl. After the game, he received more than 500 text messages, phone calls, and e-mails from friends. "This is something you dream about," Drew said.

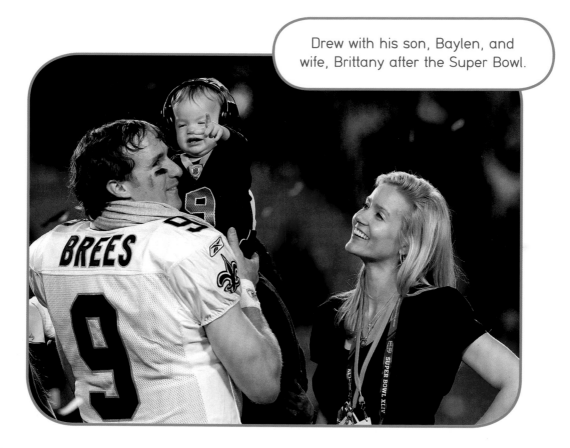

Drew with his son, Baylen, and wife, Brittany after the Super Bowl.

Drew's parents were Dallas Cowboys fans. They named their son after Dallas Cowboys receiver Drew Pearson *(number 88)*.

NEVER A DOUBT

Andrew (Drew) Christopher Brees was born January 15, 1979, in Dallas, Texas. His father, Chip, played basketball at Texas A&M University. Drew's uncle played football there. His grandfather was a high school football coach.

Drew was born with a mole on his right cheek. When he was three years old, his parents asked doctors to remove it. They said there was no medical reason to do so. The birthmark looks somewhat like a caterpillar.

In 1986, when Drew was seven, he and his family move to Austin, Texas. He played outside with his younger brother, Reid, and the neighborhood kids. "It was constant sports and activity," Drew said. "We played in the street, in the yard, using the garage as a backstop for pitching to each other."

By 1993, he was going to Westlake High School. He played football, basketball, and baseball. As a sophomore in 1994, he was the **second-string** quarterback on the **junior varsity** football team. He was behind starter Jonny Rogers. Drew knew he would be sitting on the bench. At the start of the season, he told his mother he wanted to quit. "Drew, I think you should give it more time," his mother, Mina, told him.

A few days later, Rogers was injured. Drew became the starter. In his first game, he completed nine of 10 passes for 315 yards and four touchdowns. "If Jonny hadn't gotten hurt," said coach Ron Schroeder, "I don't know if Drew would have ever had a chance." Drew led his team to an undefeated season.

Drew wasn't sure football was for him. The future Super Bowl MVP began his high school career on the bench.

As a junior, Drew led the varsity team to a 12–0–1 record. But late in the season, he injured his right knee. Drew needed surgery. Some wondered if he would recover to play football again. But Drew knew better. Soon he was running up and down hills to make his leg muscles stronger.

With Drew back at quarterback in 1996, the Westlake team, nicknamed the Chaps, went 16–0. The Chaps won the state championship. In his high school career, Drew never lost a game. Yet most colleges did not want him. "I'm a skinny, runt-looking kid," he said. "I wouldn't have [wanted] me either." Drew was thought to be too small to be a big-time college quarterback.

Purdue University offered Drew a **scholarship**. "I didn't know where the school was," he said. "I couldn't even find it on a map." Drew accepted the offer. He was on his way to West Lafayette, Indiana.

Drew had great success as a high school quarterback.

Drew did not play every game as a freshman. But Purdue coach Joe Tiller (above) knew that Drew could be special.

NATION'S FINEST

The Purdue Boilermakers play in the powerful Big Ten **Conference**. When Drew arrived in 1997, the football team was struggling to win games. Drew played in only seven games as a college freshman.

As a sophomore in 1998, Drew became a star. He set conference records in yards passing and touchdowns for a season. The Boilermakers finished with a 9–4 record. This was good enough to go to a **bowl game**. Purdue beat Kansas State in the Alamo Bowl.

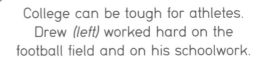
College can be tough for athletes. Drew *(left)* worked hard on the football field and on his schoolwork.

In 1999, Drew won the Socrates Award. This honor goes to a college student who does well in school and also volunteers in the community. Drew was the first winner of the award.

In his junior year, Drew led Purdue to another good record and a bowl game. He finished fourth in voting for the **Heisman Trophy**.

As a senior in 2000, Drew led Purdue to its best season in decades. In one game, the Boilermakers trailed the University of Michigan 28–10. Drew rallied his team to a last-second 32–31 win. "I'm a competitor," said Drew. "I'll never consider myself out of any game."

Purdue won the Big Ten championship. The team earned a trip to the Rose Bowl. The Boilermakers had not played in the famous bowl game since 1967. Though they lost the game to the University of Washington, Drew had helped turn his college into a winner.

Drew looks for a receiver during the Rose Bowl game.

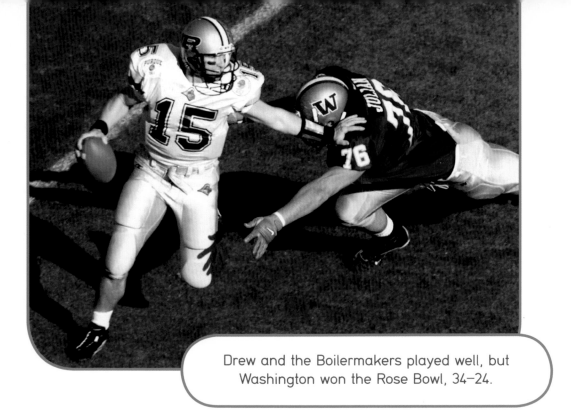

Drew and the Boilermakers played well, but Washington won the Rose Bowl, 34–24.

Drew had proved his greatness in college. But he was just six feet tall. National Football League (NFL) scouts thought he was too short. Drew was not picked in the first round of the 2001 NFL **Draft**. "People made such a big deal out of [my height]," Drew said. "I just never believed that it mattered. To play the quarterback position, it's all in the heart and the mind."

The San Diego Chargers hoped Drew would help the team return to the Super Bowl.

REBUILDING

The San Diego Chargers finally chose Drew in the second round of the 2001 draft. He was eager to prove himself. But after three seasons in the NFL, Drew and the Chargers weren't getting better. In the 2004 draft, the Chargers picked quarterback Philip Rivers. Drew feared he could lose his job. He focused harder than ever.

Drew made his first Pro Bowl team in 2004. The game was held in Honolulu, Hawaii.

Drew played so well that Rivers was kept on the bench. Drew was selected to his first **Pro Bowl** in 2004. The next year, he threw for a career-high 3,576 yards. But in the final game of the 2005 season, Denver Broncos player Gerard Warren fell on Drew's arm. "I knew it was serious the minute I got up," said Drew.

Drew's shoulder was badly hurt. He needed surgery. His arm was in a sling. Lifting the arm hurt. But Drew exercised for hours a day. "The Chargers didn't think I could come back," Drew said. "The injury was their excuse to get rid of me."

Drew is helped off the field after injuring his shoulder. He would never again play for the Chargers.

Drew became a **free agent** in 2006. He could sign a **contract** to play for any team that wanted him. The New Orleans Saints were looking for a new quarterback. The team had won just three games in 2005. Saints coach Sean Payton believed Drew's shoulder would heal. He invited Drew to visit New Orleans.

What he saw was shocking. Hurricane Katrina had destroyed much of New Orleans in 2005. "The city was devastated," Drew said. "Cars lying on the top of houses. Boats through living room windows. Unbelievable."

Drew signed a six-year deal worth $60 million to

Drew and his wife started the Brees Dream Foundation. The foundation raises money for cancer research. It also helped rebuild New Orleans after Hurricane Katrina.

New Orleans Saints coach Sean Payton *(left)* and general manager Mickey Loomis *(right)* believed in Drew. The team signed the quarterback to a huge contract.

play for the Saints. Four months after surgery, Drew was able to throw a football again. "His recovery has been one of the most remarkable of any patient I've ever treated," his doctor said.

New Orleans took on the Philadelphia Eagles in the playoffs. Drew and the Saints won the game, 27–24.

MAKING A DIFFERENCE

Drew first met with his new teammates in 2006. He led the NFL that season with 4,418 passing yards. He finished second in the voting for league MVP. The Saints beat the Philadelphia Eagles for their second playoff win in team history. They lost to the Chicago Bears the next week. But Drew had helped make the Saints winners.

Drew helped to rebuild New Orleans after Katrina. He donated millions of dollars to fix schools, playgrounds, and parks. He walked around the city looking for more ways to help. People were thankful to see him. "It's never 'Good game,' or 'Can I have your autograph?'" said Drew. "It's always somebody saying 'Thank you.'… I play football for a job. But all this, it goes way beyond football."

Drew helped rebuild New Orleans after the city was damaged by Hurricane Katrina.

In 2007, Drew set the NFL record for most completions in a season. In 2008, he became just the second quarterback ever to pass for more than 5,000 yards in a season. But the Saints missed the playoffs both years.

The 2009 season was magical for Drew and the Saints. The joy began January 15 when Drew's wife, Brittany, gave birth to their son, Baylen. What a birthday present for Drew!

In the first game of the 2009 season, Drew and the Saints crushed the Detroit Lions, 45–27.

In the 2009 season opener, Drew threw six touchdown passes against the Detroit Lions. The Saints were still unbeaten in Week 7 when they visited the Miami Dolphins. They fell behind, 24–3. Drew led an amazing comeback and ran for the winning touchdown in a 46–34 victory. The Saints finished with the best record in the conference. They crushed the Arizona Cardinals, 45–14, in the first round of the playoffs. They needed overtime to edge out the Minnesota Vikings, 31–28. The Saints were headed to the Super Bowl for the first time! Drew tied a Super Bowl record with 32 completions as the Saints became NFL champions.

Drew is on the cover of the video game Madden NFL 11. "When my son gets older, it's going to be fun to play the game together," Drew said.

Drew holds the Vince Lombardi Trophy after the Saints beat the Colts in Super Bowl XLIV.

Drew trains as hard as ever, even after winning the Super Bowl. "I focus on what it's going to take for me to become a better player and a better leader," he said. "I'm always going to try to be the best player I can be."

Selected Career Highlights

2009 Named MVP of Super Bowl XLIV
Set NFL record completion percentage (70.6)
Selected to Pro Bowl

2008 Named NFL Offensive Player of the Year
Became second quarterback in NFL history to pass for
over 5,000 yards in a season (5,069)
Selected to Pro Bowl

2007 Set NFL single-season record with 440 completions
Tied Saints single-season record with 28 touchdown passes
Set career high with 4,423 passing yards

2006 Led NFL with 4,418 passing yards
Finished second in voting for NFL MVP
Named cowinner of NFL Walter Payton Man of the Year Award
Selected to Pro Bowl

2005 Set career high with 3,576 passing yards

2004 Named NFL Comeback Player of the Year
Selected to Pro Bowl

2001 Drafted by San Diego Chargers in the second round

2000 Named Maxwell Award winner as nation's most outstanding player
Named Academic All-America Player of the Year
Named Big Ten Player of the Year
Led Purdue to a win in the Rose Bowl
Set Big Ten Conference career records in completions (1,026),
passing yards (11,792), and touchdown passes (90)
Set Big Ten single-season record for most combined passing and
rushing yards (4,189)

1999 Finalist for Davey O'Brien Award as nation's best quarterback
Named second-team All-America
Named first-team All-Big Ten
Named Purdue Male Athlete of the Year

1998 Named Big Ten Player of the Year
Set NCAA single-game record for most passing attempts (83) and
completions (55)

1996	Named Texas 5A state Player of the Year
	Led Westlake High School to undefeated season and state championship
1995	Led Westlake High School varsity to undefeated season
1994	Led Westlake High School junior varsity to undefeated season

Glossary

bowl game: one of a number of contests held after the regular season between the best college teams

conference: a group of teams

contract: a deal signed by a player and a team that states the amount of money the player is paid and the number of years he plays

draft: a yearly event in which professional teams take turns choosing new players from a group

end zone: the area beyond the goal line. To score, a team tries to get the ball into the other team's end zone.

field goal: a successful kick over the U-shaped upright poles. A field goal is worth three points.

free agent: a player who is not bound by a contract to play for a team, thereby being free to join any other team that wants him or her

Heisman Trophy: an award given yearly to the most outstanding college football player

huddle: a tight circle that football players form to talk about the next play

interception: a pass that is caught by a person on the other team. An interception results in the opposing team getting control of the ball.

junior varsity: the school team made up of less-experienced players

playoff: a series of games played after the regular season has ended

Pro Bowl: a game played after the regular season by the top players in the American Football Conference and the National Football Conference

quarterback: a player whose main job is to throw passes

scholarship: money awarded to a student to help pay college tuition

second-string: the backup or substitute players for the first-string, or starters

Super Bowl: the NFL's championship game

touchdown: a score in which the team with the ball gets into the other team's end zone

Further Reading & Websites

Kennedy, Mike, and Mark Stewart. *Touchdown: The Power and Precision of Football's Perfect Play.* Minneapolis: Millbrook Press, 2010.

Portman, Michael: *Drew Brees.* New York: Gareth Stevens Publishing, 2011.

Sandler, Michael: *Drew Brees and the New Orleans Saints: Super Bowl XLIV.* New York: Bearport Publishing, 2011.

Drew's Official Site
http://www.drewbrees.com
Drew's official website features information about his foundation to aid children of New Orleans and elsewhere, a biography of Drew, videos, games, and more.

New Orleans Saints: The Official Site
http://www.saints.com
The official website of the New Orleans Saints includes the team schedule and game results, late-breaking news, biographies of Drew Brees and other players and coaches, and much more.

Sports Illustrated Kids
http://www.sikids.com
The *Sports Illustrated Kids* website covers all sports, including football.

Index

Photo Acknowledgments

Photographs are used with the permission of: AP Photo/Paul Spinelli, p. 4;
© Larry French/Getty Images, p. 5; AP Photo/Mike Groll, p. 7; AP Photo/Kevin
Terrell, pp. 8, 28; AP Photo, p. 9; Seth Poppel Yearbook Library, pp. 11, 13; AP
Photo/Michael Conroy, File, p. 14; © Bob Leverone/The Sporting News/ZUMA
Press, p. 15; © George Long/Getty Images, p. 17; © Donald Miralle/Allsport/
Getty Images, p. 18; AP Photo/Lenny Ignelzi, p. 19; © Cal Sport Media/ZUMA
Press, p. 20; AP Photo/Denis Poroy, p. 21; AP Photo/Bill Haber, pp. 23, 25;
© Derick Hingle/Icon SMI, p. 24; © Al Messerschmidt/Getty Images, p. 26;
© Andy Lyons/Getty Images, p. 29.

Front cover: AP Photo/Kevin Terrell.